KidLit-O Presents

# What's So Great About Jane Goodall?

*A Biography of Jane Goodall Just For Kids!*

**Blake Bibbins**

**KidLit-O Books**

www.kidlito.com

© 2013. All Rights Reserved.

# Table of Contents

About KidCaps ..................................................................3

Chapter 1: Introduction............................................5

Chapter 2: The Road to Africa- Early Life and Education ...................................................................14

Chapter 3: Life in Africa – The Career of Jane Goodall......................................................................28

Chapter 4: After Africa – The Later Life of Jane Goodall......................................................................54

Chapter 5: Why Jane Goodall Is So Important 66

# About KidCaps

KidLit-O is an imprint of BookCaps™ that is just for kids! Each month BookCaps will be releasing several books in this exciting imprint. Visit are website or like us on Facebook to see more! To add your name to our mailing list, visit this link: **http://www.kidlito.com/mailing-list.html**

1

# Chapter 1: Introduction

The henhouse is quiet. As the dust floats lazily in the air and dances in the beams of light that filter in through the slats of wood on the walls, a little girl with blond hair crouches in a pile of straw in the corner and strains her eyes to see what's happening on the other side of the room. On a long shelf mounted to the wall a row of hens sit in their nest boxes, clucking contentedly and warming their eggs. The little girl shifts her weight from one leg to the other and rests her chin tiredly on her hands.

She has been waiting for her for over four hours. The knees of her dress have dirty patches from her crawling on the floor, and she is both hungry and thirsty, having missed lunch. But the promise of a new discovery is too tempting to let her even think of looking away from the animals in front of her.

One hen abruptly stands up and begins to make a different sound than it was making before. Instead of a soft clucking or quiet groaning, the hen begins to make a series of louder clucks followed by one loud crow, over and over again. It isn't long before the rest of the hens are also excitedly making the same strange squawking sound as if to encourage their fellow hen.

The little girl adjusts her position to be able to see the first hen better. The clucking all around her is distracting but also acutely hypnotizing, and the little girl begins to feel that she is about to be a part of some strange ritual that no one has ever seen before. The hen changes position so that her tail feathers are facing the girl, and something amazing begins to happen – an egg starts to peek out of the back of the chicken!

At first, the small hole under the chicken's tail feathers begins to widen, and then a soft pink muscle from inside begins to slowly emerge. The little girl holds her breath and her eyes widen as the hens all around her make an ever louder noise, getting more and more excited. She focuses all of her attention on the hen's moist egg as it is pushed out through the hole. After a few seconds of pushing, the egg falls gently to the floor of the straw-lined nest. The hen turns, looks at what she has accomplished, and then settles back down into her spot and once again starts clucking happily.

Almost as quickly as it began, the noise in the henhouse dies down and all the hens go back to making their soft noises.

Five year old Jane Goodall is amazed with what she has just seen and quickly climbs out of her hiding place in the corner of the henhouse and runs outside to find her mother and tell her everything about her astonishing discovery.

Once she finds her family, little Jane is surprised to learn that they have been searching for her, worried when no one could find her. Because Jane had spent so much time in that henhouse, trying to satisfy her curiosity about how chickens laid eggs, her mother got so worried that she phoned the police and reported her daughter missing.

But once Jane showed up, her mother simply scooped her up in her arms and held her tightly. But little Jane was too excited to be held, and wiggled out of her mother's arms so that she could look at her face to face. She began to tell her mother all about everything that she saw in the henhouse, about the noises that the hens made and about how the eggs looked as it came out of the chicken and fell into the nest. Once her mother saw how excited Jane was with what she had learned, she decided not to scold her but instead sat down with her and listened to everything that Jane had to say.

As it would turn out, Jane Goodall would have a lot to say over the years about what she learned while quietly watching animals.

From a remarkably early age, it was obvious that Jane Goodall had a passion for everything related to animals. She wanted to learn more about them and how they acted. She wanted to see how they behaved when they thought that nobody was observing them, and she was curious whether or not animals did some of the same things that people did. For Jane, every creature around her – whether a bird or a dog or a butterfly – was a marvelous new treasure box waiting to be opened, full of secrets and intriguing facts.

This passion for learning about animals would make it hard for Jane to accept the traditional role given to women in the society that she lived in. After all, Jane was born and raised in a time when women were principally expected to stay at home and raise their families, or to work as secretaries or teachers.

But from a remarkably early age, Jane Goodall wanted more from life. She wanted to travel to far-off places and to make exciting discoveries about animals. As it would turn out, Jane Goodall would have to show a lot of courage to follow her passions. And she would follow those passions to the very ends of the Earth.

She would learn things about both herself and the natural world that would forever change the way we view animals and human potential. Instead of simply living the life that everyone expected her to live, Jane Goodall would live the life that she wanted to.

Most people today know about Jane Goodall because of her incredible work with chimpanzees in the Gombe Stream National Park in Tanzania. They may also know about her efforts to educate people about environmental conservation and the need to respect animals. But what few people know is that, throughout her life, Jane Goodall has been a woman shaped by Africa. She grew up thinking about Africa; she spent her adult years observing chimpanzees and raising her son there; and now she travels the world telling everyone how important protecting the habitat of African animals is.

Jane Goodall's love for Africa has been the defining feature of her life and has given her a deep passion to do what she sees as right. Her passion for exploring the world and observing the behavior of animals has helped her to overcome incredible obstacles and to take extreme risks, even risking losing her professional reputation for the sake of learning more.

Although many years have passed since she was that little girl hiding in a henhouse to see how a chicken laid an egg, Jane Goodall still has that overwhelming sense of wonder and desire to understand the natural world around her. And thanks to her efforts, a whole new generation of men and women is looking closer at the world around them and asking the question: "Why and how does everything happen the way it does?"

But Jane Goodall's life has not been without personal sacrifice and difficult moments. Through two marriages, one ending in divorce and the other in the death of her husband, Jane has found comfort ns the force that shaped her and made her the woman she is: a love for Africa.

Jane's love for Africa began when she was just a toddler, with a truly special gift from her father.

# Chapter 2: The Road to Africa- Early Life and Education

Although Jane Goodall learned a lot of beneficial qualities from her parents, it's safe to say that she ended up choosing a remarkably different career path than either of them. Jane was born on April 3, 1934 to Mortimer Herbert Morris-Goodall and Margaret Myfanwe Joseph. Her father worked as a businessman in London, and her mother was a novelist, writing under a penname (Vanne Morris-Goodall). Although both her parents had chosen jobs that kept them sitting behind a desk and never going too far away from home, Jane would soon have bigger goals in mind. She would work behind a desk if she didn't have any other choice, but her passion would always be the outdoors.

When she was just a toddler, her father gave her a particularly special toy, one that she still keeps on her dresser today. Although some of her mother's friends were afraid that the toy would scare young Jane, her father Mortimer went ahead and gave her a stuffed chimpanzee doll anyway. Jane named it "Jubilee". Instead of being scared, it turns out that young Jane was thrilled with the gift and two quickly became inseparable.

Jane's love for animals kept growing as she got older. Her parents encouraged her young mind and made sure that she always had plenty of books to read, including ones about the study of animals (zoology) and the study of their behavior (ethology).

When she wasn't reading nature handbooks, young Jane liked to take a

2 Photo: http://www.janegoodall.ca/goodall-bio-timeline.php

notepad out into her backyard and sit and watch the neighborhood animals as they went about their business. She spent many hours observing any animals that happened to be found near her home, squatting down to see them closer, and trying to learn as many names and facts about them as she could. She would make notes and draw sketches of what she observed, always trying to learn something new.

It isn't hard to imagine why Jane enjoyed peacefully observing the animals as they went about their lives. When Jane was about five years old, Germany invaded a neighboring country and thus started World War Two in Europe. At times, it seemed that the world around young

Jane was being ripped apart at the seams and that fear and chaos were everywhere.

Great Britain (and especially Jane's hometown of London) was attacked by the Germans over and over from September 7, 1940 to May 11, 1941. The Germans sent planes and rocket bombs, destroying more than one million homes in London and killing more than 40,000 people.

Jane's father left to serve in the war and her family built a bomb shelter and had to run into it every time the German air force attacked.

The little nature observer's peaceful paradise was often interrupted by these attacks, which were called "air raids". In fact, London was attacked 71 times during the war. But even when there were no planes overhead or rocket bombs falling in her neighborhood, it was impossible for young Jane to simply forget about the war –after all, her father was away from home supporting the war effort. And her mother, sister, and she had to be careful about how much fuel and food they used from day to day.

Finally, on May 7, 1945, when Jane was nine, the German army surrendered and brought an end to World War Two in Europe. But shortly after the war, Jane experienced a sad experience closer to home when her parents divorced, and her father left the family.

Despite the big changes at home, it wasn't long before everything calmed down and Jane's life once again revolved around her studies and her one true love – observing the animals around her. Jane once described why she chose to observe animals instead of digging for old bones in a canyon. She mentioned that the desire to do so had been with her since she was a little girl:

"My childhood dream was as strong as ever–somehow I must find a way to watch free, wild animals living their own, undisturbed lives–I wanted to learn things that no one else knew, uncover secrets through patient observation. I wanted to come as close to talking to animals as I could."[3]

From the very beginning, Jane knew that she didn't want to interfere in the lives of animals or hurt them in any way – what she wanted most was to learn about animals by simply watching them.

As a child, she loved reading the book *Tarzan* and how the main character lived at peace with the animals of the jungle. However, there was just part of the story that Jane didn't like – she thought that she would make a much better wife for Tarzan than the woman (also named Jane) that he ended up with!

---

[3] Quotation source: http://tinyurl.com/lkb9afe

*Tarzan* wasn't the only book to influence young Jane Goodall - at eight years old she received the book *The Story of Dr. Doolittle* as a gift. The book, which was about a man who could converse with animals, gave Jane a brilliant idea: why not get to know more about animals right now? Why not form a club with other animal lovers?

That is how, in 1946, twelve year old Jane Goodall formed a neighborhood nature club named "The Alligator Society". The proud members of The Alligator Society included her younger sister Judy and their two friends Sally and Sue. But not just anybody could be a member of The Alligator Society. In order to join this exclusive nature club, a person had to be able to identify 10 types of dogs, 10 types of trees, 10 types of birds, and five kinds of butterflies or moths.

While she enjoyed reading books like *Tarzan* and *Dr. Doolittle*, the stories of adventures with animals had put ideas in young Jane's head. As she grew older, Jane realized that she wasn't happy anymore just holding onto a stuffed chimpanzee or observing the egrets, herons, dogs and cats in her beloved city of London. She wanted to go out into the jungle and be with *wild* animals in their natural habitat.

In other words, Jane wanted to go to Africa.

In the 1940s and 1950s, it was not common for young women to talk about having wild adventures in Africa. Most women were expected to find a good man, to get married, and then to stay home for the rest of their lives, taking care of their house or raising a family. If a woman chose to work for some reason, then a position as a secretary was one of the most common jobs available. There is no doubt that the women surrounding young Jane Goodall certainly did not talk about going out into the wild all alone and spending hours watching wild beasts.

With that in mind, how did Jane's mother, an author by trade, react when her daughter told her of her desire to go to Africa? Believe it or not, she reacted much in the same way as when little Jane had come running out of that henhouse so many years ago. Her mother Margaret didn't get upset or try to convince her daughter to change her mind. Instead, she Margaret confirmed her belief that her daughter could do anything she put her mind to, saying:

> "Jane, if you really want something, and if you work hard, take advantage of the opportunities, and never give up, you will somehow find a way."[4]

Jane's desire to go to Africa made her the person she eventually became. It

---

4    Quotation    source:    http://www.janegoodall.ca/goodall-bio-timeline.php

dominated her thoughts and hobbies as a young child and gave her a passion that few people ever find in their lives. Even though Jane would end up accepting several jobs in the meantime that had nothing to do with animals, she never lost sight of her dream of going to Africa.

In 1952, Jane finished her basic schooling. But her family (which wasn't wealthy) couldn't afford to send her to a university to continue her education. Instead of feeling sorry for herself and feeling that she would never live her dream, Jane decided to get moving and to do the best that she could on her own.

She went to a secretarial college the following year and started working as a secretary in 1954, first with her aunt and then at Oxford University. Even though she spent her days filling out and sorting documents, there was no doubt as to where Jane's true love still lay – she was allowed to bring her pet hamster, named Hamlette, to work with her each day.

Nothing, it seemed, could suppress Jane's love for animals.

The next year, 1955, Jane returned to London when she was offered a job at Schofield Productions, a company that made educational films. Jane helped to choose the music that was used in documentary films during the day, and spent her time off exploring the city of London. She took philosophy classes, and just enjoyed everything that the city had to offer.

But in May of 1956, Jane received an invitation that would change her life. Her friend, Clo Mange, invited Jane to come with her to Africa to spend some time at her family's farm. Jane recognized that this could be a prime opportunity. While she didn't necessarily want to work on an African farm, it was certainly a step closer to her goal than working on films in London.

Jane immediately quit her job at Schofield Productions and went back home to live with her mother. She got a job as a waitress and worked hard to save up enough money for the boat ticket to

Africa. And on April 2, 1957, just one day shy of her 23rd birthday, Jane Goodall stepped off of the boat *The Kenya Castle* and onto a dock in the Kenyan city of Mombasa.

Jane Goodall had arrived in Africa, the place that she had been dreaming about since she was a child. And although she wasn't too sure how long she would stay or what she would do while there, there was no doubt in her mind that everything in her life had led to this moment. Africa would become the land that would shape her as a person, and would become the place she loved the most.

5

---

5                                                                    Photo:
http://content.time.com/time/photoessays/10questions/0,30255,1
921245,00.html

# Chapter 3: Life in Africa – The Career of Jane Goodall

Jane Goodall's arrival in Kenya was not celebrated with a parade, and there weren't any important officials or scientists waiting to meet her as she stepped off the boat. The day she got to Africa, she just looked like an ordinary tourist visiting Africa.

Jane went with her friend Clo to her family's farm in the Kenyan highlands. After a while, Jane decided that she would like to stay in Africa for an extended time. But she didn't want to be a burden on anyone and make them pay for her food and drink, so she found a job working as a secretary – the same thing that she had been doing in London.

Shortly after arriving in Africa, Jane decided to write to a fellow British citizen named Louis Leakey who was born in Kenya to missionary parents. Louis was the curator of the Coryndon Museum in the capital city of Nairobi and was interested in researching as much as he could about the past of humans. He was convinced that humans evolved first in Africa and then moved to Europe, and he hoped to find proof of this by digging for fossils in Kenya.

Jane Goodall wasn't genuinely interested in looking at fossils, but she did want to take advantage of the opportunity to speak to a scientist and with someone who had spent their entire life in Africa. She hoped that Louis Leakey could tell her more about the animals of Africa.

Jane's letter to Louis Leakey ended up getting her an invitation to work for him as a secretary - an invitation which Jane quickly accepted. She spent quite a while at Louis' side as he dug up very old tools, bones, and human skulls from the Olduvai Gorge in Kenya. These findings would make Louis Leakey famous and would help convince many people in the scientific community of the theory of evolution as presented by Charles Darwin.

In the meantime, Louis Leakey talked a lot to Jane about field research that he wanted to do with the chimpanzees that lived in the nearby country of Tanzania (known back then as Tanganyika). Since the theory of evolution teaches that chimpanzees and humans had a common ancestor, Louis thought that observing chimpanzees close up could reveal a lot about what early humans were like.

But all this talk about sending someone to go watch chimpanzees was too much for Jane, and so while at work one day, Jane asked Louis to stop talking about all the research that he wanted to do. She couldn't stand hearing about someone else going to live in the wild with chimpanzees, observing them and learning about them because observing animals in their natural environment is exactly what Jane had wanted to do ever since she was a little girl.

Surprising her, Louis said, 'Jane - that is just what I had hoped you would say.' It turned out that Louis thought that Jane would be the perfect person to do the research, but he didn't want to force her to go. Louis knew that Jane had the patience, love for animals, and enough passion for the project to make it a success. More than that, because Jane hadn't gone to college, she could arrive at the park with fresh eyes and might see things that other people had missed in previous trips.

Other researchers and scientists had tried to research chimpanzees in the past, but no one was truly ever able to get a lot of new much information. Most of the visits were either too short or the groups of researchers were too large and they scared the animals away. Louise Leakey hoped that Jane could change all of that.

There was, however, one person who had learned a lot about chimps and this information would help Jane later on. It was a 1931 report published by Dr. Henry W. Nissen entitled: *A Field Study of the Chimpanzee: Observations of Chimpanzee Behavior and Environment in Western French Guinea.* Jane used the information in this report to prepare herself for her program.

Louis and Jane felt that a new way of observing the chimps was needed. Instead of a big group of researchers visiting the park for a short time, they might get better results from one researcher who could stay alone, for a long period of time. This would give the

6   Photo:   http://www.nasonline.org/publications/biographical-memoirs/memoir-pdfs/nissen-henry.pdf

chimpanzees the opportunity to get used to the researcher and eventually to accept him or her as part of their environment. A researcher like that might get to see things that had never before been observed.

Jane couldn't wait to get started.

Louis sent her back to London to get some special training in primate behavior and anatomy, and finally, on July 14, 1960, Jane Goodall arrived in the Gombe Stream National Park in Tanzania. Located on the shore of a lake, this area was home to several groups of chimpanzees that Jane would observe and protect for the rest of her life.

The country now known as Tanzania was under the control of the British at that time, and the British government did not feel comfortable sending a young woman (Jane was 26 years old) all by herself into the jungle to live with wild animals. The only way that Jane finally got permission to go was by promising to bring along her mother Margaret for the first three months.

Unfortunately, the research trip didn't start out too well. After a long ride to the lakeshore and spending awhile setting up camp, Jane walked into the jungle day after day trying to get close to the chimpanzees, always failing. Some days, she wouldn't even get to see them, but only could hear them.

One morning, Jane found a high spot that overlooked the area where the chimpanzees roamed. She could see where the apes were spending their time, but whenever she tried to get a little closer the chimpanzees would run away, terrified of this strange new creature in their territory. For several months, she could only get within about 1,500 feet of them – not nearly close enough to learn anything useful, not even using the binoculars that she had brought with her.

As if her mood wasn't bad enough, soon both Jane and her mother got sick with malaria, a dangerous disease that is transmitted through a bite from a mosquito. Both Jane and her mothers had to spend several weeks resting in bed to recover from the illness. Thankfully, both of them survived, and soon Jane was ready to get back to work.

Jane found a second group of chimpanzees to observe. Without her mother, this time, Jane decided to let the chimpanzees get used to her presence slowly, instead of walking right up to them. She explained her methods:

> "I never attempted to hide, and gradually the animals became used to the strange paleskinned primate that had invaded their territory. After about six months, most of the chimpanzees would sit and look at me calmly at distances of 100

yards. At first they fled if they saw me within 500 yards."[7]

Jane decided to show up at the same place at the same time every day so that the animals could get used to seeing her and learn that she was not a threat to them. The chimpanzees ate near the area she chose, and that is how within one year Jane earned enough of the apes' trust to get within just 30 feet of them.

Before her trip, some people had warned Jane that she would never get close enough to the chimpanzees to learn anything new. Others warned her of the incredible strength of chimpanzees and

[7] Quotation source: http://ngm.nationalgeographic.com/print/1963/08/jane-goodall/goodall-text

told her stories of people who had been injured by these strong animals.

A male chimpanzee can stand up to a height of about 5 feet 6 inches and can weigh 150 pounds (female apes are slightly smaller in size and weight). Even though they are about the same size as many human males, a chimpanzee is much stronger. Some experts say that, pound for pound, an adult chimpanzee is

---

[8] Photo: http://www.macroevolution.net/chimpanzee-pictures.html#.UpTc9sSURP8

about *twice* as strong as an adult human. So it is not hard to imagine why, although she was immensely curious, Jane decided to take her time getting to know these animals and let them get used to her little by little.

But it was not hard for Jane to be patient – that was one of the reasons why Louis Leakey thought that Jane was perfect for this project. As a child she had spent hours hiding in a dusty corner in a henhouse, and waiting to observe something incredible, so Jane Goodall knew that patience was an essential part of dealing with animals and that adapting her actions to those of the animals she was watching was the best way to be accepted by them.

Jane spent her time trying to live as the chimpanzees lived. She climbed trees with them, ate the same foods that they did, and imitated their behavior in every way she could, evening picking little bugs out of their fur.

One day, a large male chimpanzee (which she had named David Greybeard) came into her camp to get a banana that Jane had on her table. After that experience, Jane made sure that she always had plenty of bananas around to catch the attention of the apes and to make them come to her.

Within two years of arriving at the Gombe Stream National Park, Jane was delighted to see that the animals had totally accepted her presence and came to her on a regular basis looking for bananas.

Of the 100 or so chimpanzees in the park, Jane was able to get to know and observe about half of them, and she gave them names like David Greybeard, Goliath, Flo, and Frodo. She started what she called a "Banana Club", a special method for feeding the chimps bananas in her camp to make sure that they trusted her.

It wasn't long before Jane's patience and hard work paid off.

Because no one had ever taken so much time to observe chimpanzees up close and to try to be accepted by them, there were a lot of things that scientists didn't know about chimpanzees. Even though everyone guessed that chimpanzees

9    Photo:    http://ngm.nationalgeographic.com/2010/10/jane-goodall/gombe-photography#/08-jane-feeding-old-714.jpg

were similar to humans, there wasn't a lot of evidence available back then to prove how special chimpanzees actually were.

But on October 30, 1960 (just a few months after she began her field research in Gombe Park) Jane Goodall saw something that had never been observed before – she saw chimpanzees eating meat.

For a long time, animal researchers thought that chimpanzees were herbivores - creatures that only eat plants – and that they also ate small insects from time to time. But on that October day, Jane watched through her binoculars as David Greybeard sat in a tree eating something pink. She couldn't tell what the pink object was until he dropped it to the ground below, near two female chimps, and two wild pigs came running out of some nearby plants, angry and ready to fight. It was then that Jane realized that the chimpanzees were eating a baby pig that they had caught and that the parent pigs were trying to defend their babies.

No one had ever before seen chimpanzees eat meat. But this observation proved that chimpanzees were just like humans – they were omnivores, which meant that they ate both meat and plants. In fact, during her time in Gombe, Jane saw chimpanzees hunt and kill all kinds of small animals, including birds, baby baboons, insects, and other chimpanzees.

But Jane's exciting week was just beginning. On November 4, 1960, just a few days later, Jane made another surprising observation that had never before been made – she saw a chimpanzee make and use a tool.

David Greybeard was digging with his fingers in a termite mound. But what was truly astonishing was the way that David Greybeard got the termites from inside the mound and into his mouth – he used a blade of grass to pull the little bugs out of the mound.

Jane described her discovery this way:

"I was walking through the vegetation one day, and it had been raining…and then I saw this black shape, hunched over a termite mound. I peered through my binoculars, I saw a hand reach out, pick a piece of grass, and clearly was using this as a tool, pulling it out from the termite burrows into the nest and picking the termites off with his lips."[10]

What was remarkable was that not only did the chimpanzee she observed use a tool, but that he actually manufactured the tool himself. David Greybeard chose a strong piece of grass and shaped it with his hands until it was the right size, and

[10] Quotation source: http://vimeo.com/5002231

then stuck the grass into the hole he had made with his fingers in the termite mound. Any termites that grabbed onto the blade or got stuck to it were then pulled outside, where David would pick them off with his mouth.

The chimpanzee made just the right kind of tool that he needed from the materials he had available. Why was this discovery so flabbergasting? As Jane later said:

> "[Using tools] was what was supposed to make us unique at that time. 'Humans and only humans use and make tools' - we were defined as 'man the toolmaker'. And so now we have to redefine 'man',

redefine 'tool', or accept chimpanzees as human."[11]

Later on, it would be learned that the chimpanzees in Gombe used tools in at least nine different ways, including: to break hard shells, to drink water, and even to scare away other animals. Jane's discovery that chimpanzees make and use tools wholly changed the way that the world viewed both great apes and themselves.

Along with observing the intelligence of chimpanzees, Jane also discovered that they had a highly complicated social structure, and how the chimpanzees greeted each other with touches and

[11] Quotation source: http://vimeo.com/5002231

comforted each other. She also saw incredible acts of altruism – where one person does something good for another, even though it may not directly benefit them.

For example, in 1987 Jane watched as an adult female named Spindle adopted a young male chimpanzee named Mel after his mother got sick and died. There was no real reason for Spindle to do something so nice for another chimpanzee. Actually, it could have made her life more difficult. But even though it wouldn't actually help her, Spindle decided to care for Mel. This act of altruism was something that had never before been seen in apes, and this was another discovery the Jane made which changed the way that people saw these creatures.

Jane saw many heartwarming actions while in Gombe, including chimpanzees spontaneously dancing when they saw a waterfall. But Jane also learned that chimpanzees have a truly dark side. Like humans, who can both love and hate and do both wonderful thing and terrible things, Jane learned that chimpanzees were capable of both altruism and absolute cruelty.

For example, from 1974 to 1978, Jane watched as her group of chimps fought a bloody war with another group, one that led to the deaths of all of the males in the smaller group. She even saw two females kill and eat the infants of other females more than once over a period of two years and wondered whether or not she should get involved to stop the slaughter.

Jane described her feelings this way:

> "During the first ten years of the study I had believed […] that the Gombe chimpanzees were, for the most part, rather nicer than human beings. […] Then suddenly we found that chimpanzees could be brutal—that they, like us, had a darker side to their nature." [12]

These surprising observations helped Jane to get more funding for her

[12] Quotation source: http://tinyurl.com/lskxf5r

research, and eventually, *National Geographic* magazine took an interest in her work. They wanted her to write about her experiences and observations in Gombe, so in August 1962 they sent a photographer named Hugo van Lawick to Gombe to take pictures of Jane and her work. Jane's first article, entitled "My Life among Wild Chimpanzees", came out in the August 1963 issue of *National Geographic* magazine.

So far, Africa had been everything that Jane had hoped it would be. It gave her an opportunity to get closer to majestic wild animals and to observe behaviors that no one else had ever observed. The world was starting to take notice of Jane's work and to appreciate how wondrous chimpanzees really were and much there was to learn about them.

It was also in 1962 that Louis Leakey convinced Jane to apply for a PhD degree from Cambridge University (even though she didn't even have a Bachelor's Degree). Louis knew that Jane would continue to get the world's attention for her work in Gombe, and knew that the scientific community would take her more seriously if she had a degree from Cambridge. Jane was accepted into the program in 1962, and spent the next few years travelling back and forth from Gombe to Cambridge, working to earn her degree while staying as long as she could in Gombe each trip to observe the chimpanzees.

Jane's time in Cambridge was uncomfortable at times as fellow researchers criticized her methods as "unscientific". They said that Jane broke several important rules of research in her time at Gombe, like giving the chimpanzees names instead of numbers or interacting with the animals instead of keeping her distance. Some people even went so far as to say that the bananas Jane gave the chimpanzees caused the wars and aggression that she observed.

Despite the negative attention she got, Jane earned her PhD in ethology (study of animal behavior) from Cambridge in 1965 and soon after returned permanently to her beloved Africa to focus on studying chimpanzees.

That same year, the National Geographic society gave her enough money to be able to build aluminum buildings at Gombe. These simple buildings were the first permanent structures in the area (everyone had been living in tents up till then), and with their construction the Gombe Stream Research Centre was officially born.

But Africa did much more for Jane Goodall than simply advance her career. Africa changed Jane Goodall's personal life, as well.

After spending many long weeks and months working with Hugo van Lawick, the photographer sent by *National Geographic*, Jane and he fell in love and were married in London on March 28, 1964. A few years later, on March 4, 1967 Jane gave birth in Nairobi to their son, which they named Hugo Eric Louis (although he often went by the loving nickname "Grub").

Ever since she was a little girl, Jane Goodall had dreamed of a life in Africa, where she could observe wild animals in their natural habitat. By 1967, 33 year old Jane was doing exactly that. The goal that had shaped her as a young woman had finally been realized, and now that she was working side by side with her husband and caring for her dear son she realized that she wouldn't have either of them in her life if it wouldn't have been if she hadn't accepted the invitation to visit Kenya.

The observations of Jane Goodall shook the scientific community and got all kinds of people more interested in chimpanzees and their behavior. Children and adults alike loved hearing about the discoveries made by this passionate researcher.

By the 1980s, Jane Goodall had established herself as an expert on chimpanzee behavior and had taught the world many new things. But her work would soon take on a new sense of urgency, even as her personal life saw great changes.

# Chapter 4: After Africa – The Later Life of Jane Goodall

As Jane continued her work at Gombe, now with her son by her side, she got the opportunity to publish more of her observations in different books and magazines. Along with writing several articles for *National Geographic* magazine, Jane also wrote several books both by herself and with co-authors.

For example, in 1971 she wrote the book *In the Shadow of Man*, where she described in great detail her experiences in Tanzania, beginning with her arrival at Gombe National Park. She talked about some of her most exciting discoveries and what it was like to learn about the park's chimpanzees by making herself a part of their daily activities.

In the meantime, her son Grub continued to grow older, surrounded each day by the jungle and its wildlife. In fact, Grub's proud parents made a book about him, with Jane's words and Hugo's pictures. The book, titled *Grub, the Bush Baby*, came out in 1988 and made every child who read it jealous that they weren't raised in the jungle like Grub was.

But while Jane's professional life continued to flourish and she got more and more attention for her work, her personal life started to run into some difficulties. Her husband, Hugo, was still working as a photographer and as a filmmaker, travelling all over Africa for his projects. For her part, Jane was very busy in Gombe, observing the chimpanzees, caring for their son, and travelling to the United States twice a year to teach. She also made memorable appearances to educate people about the chimpanzees of Tanzania.

But after about ten years of marriage, it was clear that Jane and Hugo were both too committed to their individual careers to be able to hold their family together. So in 1974, they decided that the best thing would be to get a divorce while staying friends. And, in fact, they were able to keep in touch with each other throughout the years until Hugo died in 2002.

In February of 1975, Jane got married for a second time, to a man named Derek Bryceson, a local politician and director of Tanzania's national parks. The marriage was a singularly happy one, with both husband and wife working hard to protect the chimpanzee habitats in Tanzania.

The same year that she got married for the second time (1975), Jane experienced the shock of a lifetime: the lives of several researchers who had joined her at the Gombe facility were put in danger. But the dangerous creature wasn't a chimpanzee this time – it was man.

On May 19, 1975, three dozen rebel fighters from the nearby country of Zaire (now known as the Democratic Republic of Congo) snuck into the Gombe camp in the middle of the night and kidnapped four of the researchers working with Jane. Three of them were students from Stanford University in California, and one was a researcher from the Netherlands. All four of them were carried across the lake to the rebels' camp, where they were given little food and forced to live in cramped huts on the beach.

Jane herself narrowly avoided being captured by the rebels after she was warned by a local villager that had seen the soldiers coming.

Jane and her colleagues thought that they would never see the four kidnapped researchers again, but then they received ransom notes, asking for $500,000 and weapons so that the rebels could keep fighting the war against their government. It took two long months, but finally the ransom money was paid, and the victims were released, after having been mistreated for several weeks.

After the kidnapping, the government of Tanzania told Jane that she could not return to Gombe for a while because it was too dangerous; the rebels might come back and try to kidnap other foreigners so they could get more money. So for several months, Jane stayed with her new husband in his home in the city of Dar es Salaam, the largest city in Tanzania.

Two years later, Jane formed a very special organization called "The Jane Goodall Institute for Wildlife Research, Education and Conservation". The institute went on to establish offices all around the world to focus on educating people about great apes; how to protect them both in the wild and in captivity. Although she still spent a lot of her time with the chimpanzees in Gombe and teaching in universities, Jane was trying to use her energy to make positive changes in more than just one area.

Jane's life was terribly busy, but was also very satisfying and kept her happy. But in

October of 1980, tragedy struck Jane Goodall's life again.

After just five years of marriage, Jane's second husband, Derek Bryceson, died after a fight with cancer. Jane was terribly sad, and for a quite a while she felt very alone and abandoned. One of the things that brought her comfort was going back to Gombe and watching her beloved chimpanzees.

For several years after the death of Derek, Jane focused on her research at Gombe. She loved seeing the animals in the wild, happy and healthy. While she knew that there were people who killed female chimps and sold the babies illegally and that laboratories around the world used chimpanzees in their medical research, Jane put those problems into the back of her mind just tried to do what she could to help the chimps living in Tanzania. She tried to protect them and their habitat the best she could.

But all of that changed in 1986, the year that Jane Goodall became a true outspoken conservationist.

Two things happened in 1986 that made Jane Goodall decide to use her voice and influence to help conserve and protect great apes around the world.

First, she attended a conference based on her book (also released that year) titled *The Chimpanzees of Gombe:*

*Patterns of Behaviour.* One expert after another warned the audience how quickly the jungle habitats in Africa that chimpanzees lived in were disappearing. Jane had known that humans were moving into more and more areas that animals used to dominate, but she had no idea of how bad the situation really was. She was moved to act.

Then something else happened that year. Animal activists (people who fight to protect animals) broke into a laboratory that used chimpanzees to conduct research. They took video of the chimpanzee cages, which were very small, and sent the video to Jane at Gombe. She was absolutely shocked by what she saw.

She described seeing the eyes of the young chimps in the cages as if they were the eyes of orphaned refugee children in Africa – they had no hope in them. After touring one of the facilities in person a short time later, Jane left the laboratory in tears once she saw with her own eyes how the chimpanzees were living.

Those two events – the conference that mentioned the disappearing habitat and the video from the laboratory – both convinced Jane to let others do the research at Gombe. From that moment on, she felt that she should spend her time traveling the world, talking to influential decision makers, and educating everyone she could about the dangers that chimpanzees and other great apes were facing.

By 1995, Jane Goodall could say this about her life since 1986: "During the past nine years, the longest I've spent in any one place has been three weeks." Today, she still lives mainly on the road, travelling about 300 days per year, usually attending multiple lectures and meetings per day.

In particular, Jane spends her time making sure that children understand the importance of protecting both the environment and the animals that live there. Her organization "Roots and Shoots" was formed in 1991 and helps young people to improve their communities on the local level.

13

Jane's efforts have helped to make some real changes. Most laboratories now give their chimpanzees better living conditions, both during and after their time as test subjects. Countries around the world are taking seriously their responsibility to protect the jungles where great apes live.

13    Photo:    http://rootsandshoots.org/news/three-young-leaders-jane-goodall%E2%80%99s-roots-shoots-accompany-grand-marshal-dr-jane-goodall-rose

And Jane has even helped to establish specific centers in countries like Kenya, Uganda, Congo, and Burundi to care for orphaned chimps whose mothers were killed by hunters.

Since her time in Africa, many governments and organizations around the world have recognized the significant work of Jane Goodall. For example, she has received a lifetime achievement award from the "In Defense of Animals" group and was named Anthropologist of the Year in 1989. On April 16, 2002, she was appointed by the Secretary-General of the United Nations to serve as a United Nations Messenger of Peace, and was made a Dame of the British Empire (which is the same as being named a knight, but for women) on February 20, 2004.

Jane's life has changed a lot since she stopped spending so much time at Gombe, but her passion for animals and seeing them live happily in their natural habitat has not.

# Chapter 5: Why Jane Goodall Is So Important

Jane Goodall is a woman that has been shaped by Africa. Although her work has focused mainly on great apes and their behavior, her observations have affected every person living on the planet today, forcing them to rethink all that they have been told about themselves and the animals that share the planet with them. In many ways, both Jane's personal life and her work have been exemplary.

For example, Jane has been a special example for women who have an interest in science. Born at a time when women were not expected to have inquisitive minds and to want to trek off into the jungles of the world, Jane proved that a woman can be an excellent researcher. Even though she had to climb trees, survive being hit and dragged by often aggressive chimpanzees, and endure the extreme temperatures and rainy storms of Tanzania, Jane never abandoned her field research assignment. Her example opened the door for many female researchers in different parts of the world to live out their dreams, as well.

Jane was able to learn so much about her subjects because she got close to them and treated them as individuals, and thus she set a good example for researchers. While some professionals may not like the idea of Jane naming the chimpanzees and seeing them as people, her doing so allowed her to see the culture and sense of community that existed in the group. She was able to see how family connections affected the actions of the apes and how each animal had its own distinct personality that guided the way it behaved. It was only by living as the chimps lived and seeing them as individuals was Jane Goodall able to learn so much about their behavior.

Finally, Jane was and is an example to every human living today. Her passion for animals and for their protection has taught people in many nations about the importance of respecting both animals and their habitats. Jane has also taught young people to be inquisitive about their environment and to ask questions about the things that they see, inspiring those same young people to act in order to make their communities better places.

If Jane Goodall had never been born, or if she had chosen to stay in London as work as a secretary, there is so much that we wouldn't know about chimpanzees today. Instead of seeing them as intelligent, often compassionate creatures that can use tools and show altruism we would see them as big dumb animals not worth protecting.

Whether or not we agree with the theory of evolution, which teaches that humans and chimpanzees are related, there can be no doubt that Jane Goodall has shown us that chimpanzees are special animals which deserve to be treated with dignity and to be protected.

Jane Goodall was shaped by Africa. As a young girl, the stories she read in the book *Tarzan* and the stuffed chimpanzee her father gave her sparked her interest in this continent. As she grew older, her love for animals only increased and she never stopped thinking about Africa. It defined her childhood.

As a young woman, she finally got an opportunity to travel to the land of her dreams. She boarded a boat to Kenya, and soon found herself giving bananas to chimps like David Greybeard and observing things the chimpanzees did that no one else had ever observed. She met both of her husbands in Africa and had her only child there. And it was in Africa that she decided how to she would spend the rest of her life – helping to conserve wild animals and their habitats.

Today, more than 50 years have passed since Jane first arrived at Gombe Stream national Park in Tanzania, and her life still revolves around Africa. She talks about it with every speech she gives and with every word she writes. She cherishes the memories she made there and can reflect on the legacy that she left in Gombe that other researchers are carrying on.

Jane still goes back to Africa every chance that she gets.

That young girl who crouched in the pile of straw in the corner of a hen house has grown up into a woman who still believes in patiently waiting. Because there are still so many unanswered questions about the natural world, Jane Goodall keeps patiently watching and observing, watching for something amazing to happen.

14

[14] Photo: http://foglobe.com/data_images/main/jane-goodall/jane-goodall-04.jpg

CPSIA information can be obtained
at www.ICGtesting.com
Printed in the USA
FSOW02n0712280316
18523FS